enVision™ Geometry
Assessment Readiness
Workbook

Pearson
Boston, Massachusetts

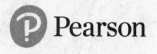

ISBN-13: 978-0-328-93170-5
ISBN-10:   0-328-93170-5

Contents

enVision™ Geometry

Standards Practice: Weeks 1–30

Practice Test A

Practice Test B

Practice Test C

Progress Monitoring Chart

Reference Sheets

Standards Practice Week 1

Selected Response

1. What is the midpoint of the line segment connecting (–2, 6) and (4, 14)?

Ⓐ (1, 4)

Ⓑ (3, 10)

Ⓒ (1, 10)

Ⓓ (2, 8)

Constructed Response

2. Construct $\overline{AB}$ so that $CD + EF = AB$.

C D

E F

Extended Response

3. $\angle ABC$ and $\angle CBD$ are supplementary angles. $m\angle ABC = (5x + 12)°$ and $m\angle CBD = (13x + 24)°$.

a. Find x.

b. Find $m\angle ABC$ and $m\angle CBD$.

c. Show how you can check your answer.

Standards Practice Week 2

Selected Response

1. Is the following statement true? If it is false, choose a correct counterexample.

   If a number is prime, then it is odd.

   (A) True

   (B) False; 4 is even.

   (C) False; 15 is odd.

   (D) False; 2 is even.

2. What appears to be the next two terms in the sequence?

   b, e, h, k, n,…

   (A) q, t   (C) q, s

   (B) o, p   (D) n, q

Constructed Response

3. Use the Law of Detachment to draw a conclusion. If it is not possible, then state why.

   If you receive a score greater than 75, then you pass the class.

   You received a score of 82.

Extended Response

4. Use the following statement.

   If the three sides of a triangle have the same length, the triangle is equilateral.

   a. What is the inverse of the statement?

   b. What is the converse of the statement?

   c. What can you conclude with the following statement using the Law of Syllogism?

   If a triangle is equilateral, then each angle of the triangle measures 60°.

Standards Practice Week 3

Selected Response

1. To write an indirect proof of the following statement, what should the assumption be?

   If a whole number is between 8 and 10, then it is a factor of 360.

   Ⓐ A whole number is not between 8 and 10.

   Ⓑ A whole number is not a factor of 360.

   Ⓒ A whole number is a factor of 360.

   Ⓓ A whole number is between 8 and 10.

Constructed Response

2. What is the value of x?

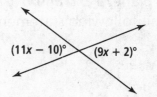

$(11x - 10)°$ $(9x + 2)°$

Extended Response

3. Given $JK = KL$, $JK = 4x + 12$, and $JL = 60$, prove that $x = 4.5$.

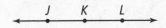

Fill in the blanks using the following reasons.

- Transitive Property of Equality
- Substitution Property
- Given
- Division Property of Equality

Statement	Reason
1) $JK = KL$, $JL = 45$	1) _____
2) $JK = 4x + 12$	2) Vertical Angles Theorem
3) $KL = 4x + 12$	3) _____
4) $JL = JK + KL$	4) Segment Addition Postulate
5) $JL = 4x + 12 + 4x + 12$	5) _____
6) $JL = 8x + 24$	6) Combine like terms.
7) $8x + 24 = 60$	7) Transitive Property of Equality
8) $8x = 36$	8) Subtraction Property
9) $x = 4.5$	9) _____

Standards Practice Week 4

Selected Response

1. Lines a, b, and c are in the same coordinate plane. $a \perp b$ and $b \perp c$. Which of the following statements is true?

   Ⓐ $a \parallel c$

   Ⓑ $a \perp c$

   Ⓒ $b \parallel c$

   Ⓓ $a \parallel b$

Constructed Response

2. $\angle A$ and $\angle B$ are alternate interior angles formed by two parallel lines and a transversal. $m\angle A = (3x - 8)°$ and $m\angle B = 88°$. Find x.

Extended Response

3. Prove that $r \parallel s$ if $\angle 1$ and $\angle 7$ are supplementary by writing the correct reason in the appropriate place.

   Fill in the blanks using the following reasons.

   - Substitution Property
   - Converse of the Same-Side Interior Angles Postulate
   - Vertical Angles Theorem

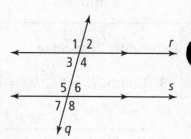

Statement	Reason
1) $\angle 1$ and $\angle 7$ are supplementary.	1) Given
2) $\angle 1 \cong \angle 4$	2) Vertical Angles Theorem
3) $\angle 4$ and $\angle 7$ are supplementary.	3) _____
4) $\angle 7 \cong \angle 6$	4) _____
5) $\angle 4$ and $\angle 6$ are supplementary.	5) Substitution Property
6) $r \parallel s$	6) _____

Name _____

Standards Practice Week 5

Selected Response

1. Which equation when graphed is a line perpendicular to the line with equation $y = 5(x - 1)$?

Ⓐ $y = \frac{1}{5}(x - 1)$

Ⓑ $x + 5y = 15$

Ⓒ $y = 5x + 8$

Ⓓ $5x - y = 10$

Constructed Response

2. In $\triangle ABC$, $m\angle A = 27°$, $m\angle B = x°$, and $m\angle C = 2x°$. Find $m\angle B$ and $m\angle C$.

Extended Response

3. Consider $\triangle ABC$. The exterior angles of $\triangle ABC$ are $\angle 1$, $\angle 2$, and $\angle 3$, respectively. Prove that the sum of the measures of the exterior angles of the triangle is 360°. Use the reasons below to complete the proof. Some reasons may be used more than once.

- Linear Pairs Theorem
- Triangle Angle-Sum Theorem
- Definition of linear pair
- Subtraction Property of Equality
- Addition Property of Equality
- Substitution Property

Statement	Reason
1) $\triangle ABC$ with exterior angles $\angle 1$, $\angle 2$, and $\angle 3$.	1) Given
2) $\angle 1$ and $\angle A$ are a linear pair.	2) Definition of linear pair
3) $m\angle 1 + m\angle A = 180°$	3) _____
4) $\angle 2$ and $\angle B$ are a linear pair.	4) Definition of linear pair
5) $m\angle 2 + m\angle B = 180°$	5) _____
6) $\angle 3$ and $\angle C$ are a linear pair.	6) Definition of linear pair
7) $m\angle 3 + m\angle C = 180°$	7) _____
8) $m\angle 1 + m\angle A + m\angle 2 + m\angle B + m\angle 3 + m\angle C = 540°$	8) _____
9) $m\angle A + m\angle B + m\angle C = 180°$	9) _____
10) $m\angle 1 + m\angle 2 + m\angle 3 + 180° = 540°$	10) _____
11) $m\angle 1 + m\angle 2 + m\angle 3 = 360°$	11) _____

Standards Practice Week 6

Selected Response

1. What are the coordinates of the image $R_{x\text{-axis}}(-3, 8)$?

   Ⓐ $(8, -3)$

   Ⓑ $(3, 8)$

   Ⓒ $(3, -8)$

   Ⓓ $(-3, -8)$

Constructed Response

2. a. What are the coordinates of the vertices of $T_{\langle -5, -4\rangle}(ABCD)$?

   b. Graph the image of $ABCD$.

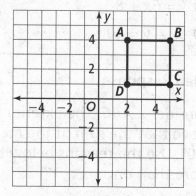

Extended Response

3. a. Plot the points $A(-4, 1)$, $B(-2, 4)$, and $C(-1, 0)$.

   b. Graph the image of $\triangle ABC$ after the given transformation. Let ℓ be the line with equation $x = -2$.

   $(R_{y\text{-axis}} \circ R_\ell)(\triangle ABC)$

   c. Describe another transformation that will make the same image.

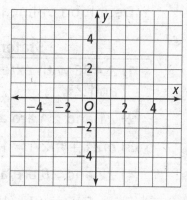

Standards Practice Week 7

Selected Response

1. What are the coordinates of the image $r_{(270°,\ O)}(-4,\ 5)$?

Ⓐ $(5,\ -4)$

Ⓑ $(-5,\ 4)$

Ⓒ $(5,\ 4)$

Ⓓ $(-5,\ -4)$

Constructed Response

2. a. What are the coordinates of the vertices of $(T_{\langle 0,\ -5\rangle} \circ R_{y\text{-axis}})(ABCD)$?

b. Graph the image of *ABCD*.

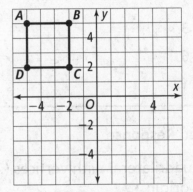

Extended Response

3. a. Plot the points $A(2,\ -1)$, $B(5,\ -4)$, and $C(1,\ -3)$.

b. Graph the image of $\triangle ABC$ after the given transformation.

$(R_{y\text{-axis}} \circ R_{x\text{-axis}})(\triangle ABC)$

c. Describe another transformation that will make the same image.

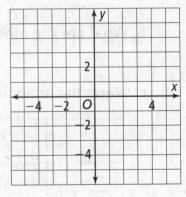

Name _____

Standards Practice Week 8

Selected Response

1. How many lines of symmetry does the regular hexagon shown have?

    Ⓐ 2

    Ⓑ 3

    Ⓒ 6

    Ⓓ 12

Constructed Response

2. What types of symmetry does the figure show?

Extended Response

3. A quadrilateral with vertices (2, 5) and (−3, −4) has point symmetry about the origin.

    a. What transformation maps the quadrilateral onto itself?

    b. What are the other two vertices of the quadrilateral?

    c. Graph the quadrilateral.

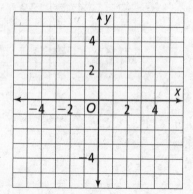

Standards Practice Week 9

Selected Response

1. In the diagram shown, which congruence transformation shows that $\triangle ABC \cong \triangle XYZ$?

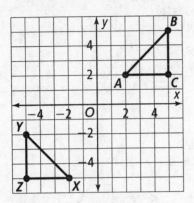

Ⓐ $T_{\langle 0, -7 \rangle} \circ R_{y\text{-axis}}$

Ⓑ $T_{\langle -7, 0 \rangle} \circ R_{x\text{-axis}}$

Ⓒ $R_{y\text{-axis}} \circ R_{x\text{-axis}}$

Ⓓ $R_{x\text{-axis}} \circ r_{(90°, O)}$

Constructed Response

2. What is $m\angle DAB$?

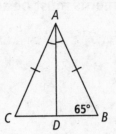

Extended Response

3. The diagram shows 4 triangles.

   a. Which triangles are congruent to $\triangle ABC$?

   b. Describe the transformations that map $\triangle ABC$ to each congruent triangle.

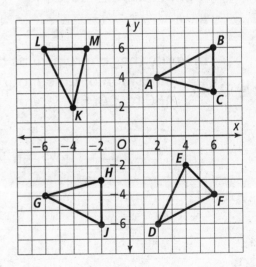

Standards Practice Week 10

Selected Response

1. If $\triangle LMN \cong \triangle PQR$, which of the following statements must be true?

   (A) $\overline{NM} \cong \overline{RQ}$

   (B) $\overline{LN} \cong \overline{PQ}$

   (C) $\overline{LN} \cong \overline{QR}$

   (D) $\overline{MN} \cong \overline{PQ}$

Constructed Response

2. For each pair of triangles, state which theorem can be used to show that the triangles are congruent.

   a.

   b.

   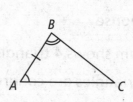 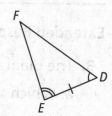

Extended Response

3. a. Which theorem can be used to show that $\triangle ABC \cong \triangle BEF$?

   b. Verify the congruence by describing a composition of rigid motions to map $\triangle ABC$ to $\triangle DEF$.

Name _____

Standards Practice Week 11

Selected Response

1. Which of the following statements is true?

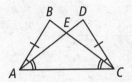

Ⓐ By SSS, $\triangle ABC = \triangle CDA$.

Ⓑ By HL, $\triangle ABC = \triangle CDA$.

Ⓒ By SAS, $\triangle ABC = \triangle CDA$.

Ⓓ There is not enough information to show that $\triangle ABC = \triangle CDA$.

Constructed Response

2. For what values of x and y are the triangles congruent by the Hypotenuse-Leg Theorem?

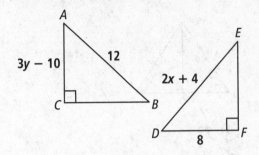

Extended Response

3. **Given:** $\overline{SU} \cong \overline{TU}$, $\angle UWV \cong \angle UVW$

Prove: $\triangle SVW \cong \triangle TWV$

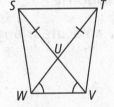

Fill in the blanks using the following reasons.

- AAS
- Converse of the Isosceles Triangle Theorem
- CPCTC
- SAS
- Vertical Angles Theorem

Statement	Reason
1) $\overline{SU} \cong \overline{TU}$, $\angle UWV \cong \angle UVW$	1) Given
2) $\angle SUW \cong \angle TUV$	2) _____
3) $\overline{WU} \cong \overline{VU}$	3) _____
4) $\triangle SUW \cong \triangle TUV$	4) _____
5) $\angle WSU \cong \angle VTU$	5) _____
6) $\overline{WV} \cong \overline{VW}$	6) Reflexive Property of Congruence
7) $\triangle SVW \cong \triangle TWV$	7) _____

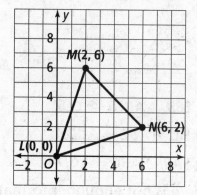

Standards Practice Week 12

Selected Response

1. $\overline{BD}$ is the perpendicular bisector of $\overline{AC}$. If $AB = 4x + 12$, $AC = 72$, and $BC = 64$, what is the value of x?

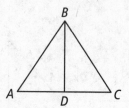

- Ⓐ 17
- Ⓑ 15
- Ⓒ 13
- Ⓓ 8

Constructed Response

2. What are the coordinates of the orthocenter of △*LMN*?

Extended Response

3. a. Draw an acute triangle, and construct the inscribed and circumscribed circle.

   b. Describe your method.

Standards Practice Week 13

Selected Response

1. Which set of lengths could not be the side lengths of a triangle?

   Ⓐ 5, 2, 6

   Ⓑ 12, 18, 9

   Ⓒ 52, 30, 28

   Ⓓ 60, 12, 48

Constructed Response

2. Suppose $BC > DE > CD$. Write an inequality describing the possible values of x.

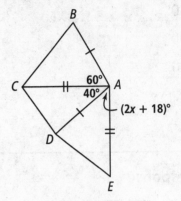

Extended Response

3. **a.** Write an inequality describing the possible values of x for $\triangle PQR$.

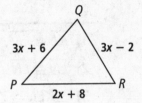

   b. Write an inequality describing the possible values of x for $\triangle STU$.

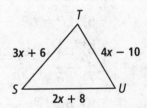

   c. Suppose $m\angle S < m\angle P$. Write an inequality describing the possible values of x.

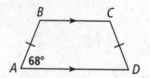
Standards Practice Week 14

Selected Response

1. What is the sum of the interior angle measures of a convex dodecagon (12-gon)?

   Ⓐ 2,160°

   Ⓑ 1,800°

   Ⓒ 1,440°

   Ⓓ 360°

Constructed Response

2. Quadrilateral *ABCD* is an isosceles trapezoid. What are $m\angle B$, $m\angle C$, and $m\angle D$?

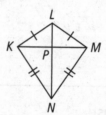

Extended Response

3. Given: $\overline{KL} \cong \overline{LM}$, $\overline{MN} \cong \overline{KN}$

   Prove: $\overline{KP} \cong \overline{MP}$, $\overline{KM} \perp \overline{LN}$

   Fill in the blanks to complete the proof.

Statement	Reason
1) $\overline{KL} \cong \overline{LM}$, $\overline{MN} \cong \overline{KN}$	1) Given
2) $\overline{LN} \cong \overline{LN}$	2) _____
3) $\triangle KLN \cong \triangle MLN$	3) _____
4) $\angle KLP \cong \angle MLP$	4) _____
5) $\overline{LP} \cong \overline{LP}$	5) _____
6) $\triangle KLP \cong \triangle MLP$	6) _____
7) $\overline{KP} \cong \overline{MP}$, $\angle LPK \cong \angle LPM$	7) _____
8) $m\angle LPK + m\angle LPM = 180°$	8) _____
9) $m\angle LPK = m\angle LPM = 90°$	9) _____
	_____
10) $\overline{KM} \perp \overline{LN}$	10) _____

Standards Practice Week 15

Selected Response

1. Quadrilateral *FGHK* is a parallelogram. Which statement is not necessarily true?

    Ⓐ $\angle FKG \cong \angle HGK$

    Ⓑ $\angle FGK \cong \angle HGK$

    Ⓒ $\angle GFH \cong \angle FHK$

    Ⓓ $\angle FGH \cong \angle FKH$

Constructed Response

2. Solve to find the values of *x* and *y* in the parallelogram.

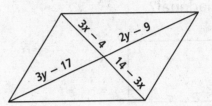

Extended Response

3. **Given:** $\overline{AC}$ and $\overline{BD}$ bisect each other.

    Prove: *ABCD* is a parallelogram.

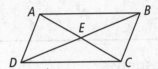

Standards Practice Week 16

Selected Response

1. In rectangle *PQRS*, *PR* = 3*x* − 9 and *QS* = 5*x* − 25. What is the length of a diagonal?

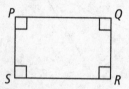

- (A) 24
- (B) 16
- (C) 15
- (D) 8

Constructed Response

2. Suppose $m\angle 1 = (3x - 15)°$ and $m\angle 2 = (105 - 5y)°$. Solve to find the values of *x* and *y* so parallelogram *ABCD* is a rhombus.

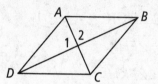

Extended Response

3. **Given:** $\overline{WXYZ}$ is a parallelogram.
   $\overline{WY}$ bisects ∠*XYZ*.

   Prove: $\overline{WY}$ bisects ∠*ZWX*.

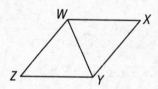

Name _____

Standards Practice Week 17

Selected Response

1. Is $D_{(n,\ P)}(\triangle PQR) = \triangle P'Q'R'$ an enlargement or reduction? What is the scale factor n of the dilation?

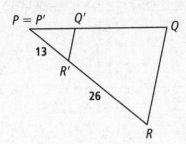

Ⓐ enlargement; $n = 2$

Ⓑ enlargement; $n = 3$

Ⓒ reduction; $n = \frac{1}{3}$

Ⓓ reduction; $n = \frac{1}{2}$

Constructed Response

2. Quadrilateral $ABCD$ has vertices $A(-2, 4)$, $B(1, 4)$, $C(4, -3)$, and $D(-1, -3)$.

a. Graph $ABCD$.

b. Graph $D_3(ABCD)$.

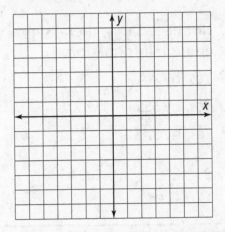

Extended Response

3. a. Is $\triangle ABC \sim \triangle DEF$? If so, describe a similarity transformation that maps $\triangle ABC$ to $\triangle DEF$. If not, explain.

b. Is $\triangle ABC \sim \triangle GJH$? If so, describe a similarity transformation that maps $\triangle ABC$ to $\triangle GJH$. If not, explain.

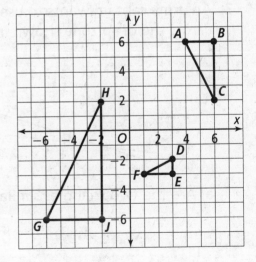

Name _____

Standards Practice Week 18

Selected Response

1. Are the triangles similar? If so, choose the reasoning.

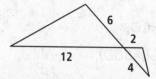

Ⓐ Not necessarily; there is not enough information.

Ⓑ Yes, by AA ~

Ⓒ Yes, by SSS ~

Ⓓ Yes, by SAS ~

Constructed Response

2. **a.** Explain why △ABC ~ △DBE.

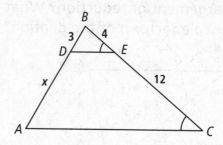

b. Solve for the value of x.

Extended Response

3. An army captain wants to use similar triangles to determine the distance d across the drop zone shown in the diagram.

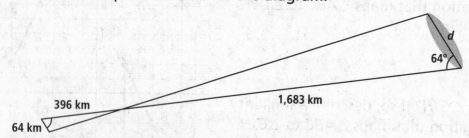

a. Are the two triangles similar? Explain.

b. What is the distance across the drop zone?

Standards Practice Week 19

Selected Response

1. Point *D* is the midpoint of $\overline{AC}$, point *E* is the midpoint of $\overline{AB}$, and *DE* = 8. What is *BC*?

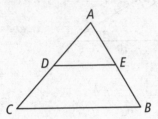

Ⓐ 4

Ⓑ 8

Ⓒ 16

Ⓓ 24

Constructed Response

2. a. What is the value of *x*?

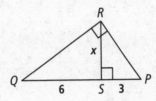

b. What are *QR* and *PR*?

Extended Response

3. Use the diagram to answer the questions.

a. Suppose *AB* = 8, *AC* = 6, and *CE* = 12. What is *BE*? Explain using the Triangle Angle-Bisector Theorem.

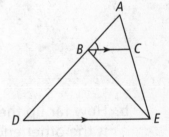

b. Suppose *AB* = 8, *BD* = 16, and *AC* = 6. What is *CE*? Explain using the Side-Splitter Theorem.

c. Explain why $\overline{BD} \cong \overline{BE}$.

Name _____

Standards Practice Week 20

Selected Response

1. What is the value of *s*?

12

s

Ⓐ $3\sqrt{2}$

Ⓑ 6

Ⓒ $6\sqrt{2}$

Ⓓ 12

Constructed Response

2. Find the values of *d* and *x* to the nearest tenth.

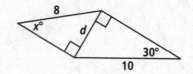

8

x°

d

30°

10

Extended Response

3. A 9-ft ladder is leaning against a wall and makes a 55° angle with the ground.

  a. Make and label a diagram to model this scenario.

  b. How far up the wall is one end of the ladder? How far away from the wall is the other end? Round to the nearest tenth.

  c. Verify your answers using the Pythagorean Theorem.

Standards Practice Week 21

Selected Response

1. What is the area of the triangle to the nearest square inch?

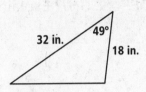

Ⓐ 189 in.^{2}

Ⓑ 217 in.^{2}

Ⓒ 331 in.^{2}

Ⓓ 435 in.^{2}

Constructed Response

2. An outfielder catches a fly ball. Her distance to the shortstop is 75 ft, as shown in the diagram. If she is 150 ft away from the first baseman, what is the value of x? Round to the nearest tenth.

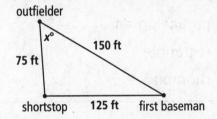

Extended Response

3. A ship has sailed 520 mi from the port in Jacksonville. From the ship, the captain records an angle measurement between the port in Jacksonville and the port at a private island as 52°. He knows the angle from the port in Jacksonville between the ship and the island port is 78°.

   a. Make and label a diagram to model this scenario.

   b. To the nearest mile, how far is the ship from the island port? Explain.

Standards Practice Week 22

Selected Response

1. What is the most precise name for the quadrilateral defined by the following points in the coordinate plane?

$A(2, -5)$, $B(2, 0)$, $C(-2, 3)$, $D(-2, -2)$

Ⓐ kite

Ⓑ parallelogram

Ⓒ rectangle

Ⓓ rhombus

Constructed Response

2. Consider the points $D(1, 5)$, $E(5, 8)$, $F(-3, 8)$, $G(-3, 1)$, $H(1, 4)$, and $J(-7, 4)$. Is $\triangle DEF \cong \triangle GHJ$? Explain.

Extended Response

3. The diagram shown is used to prove that a parallelogram with perpendicular diagonals is a rhombus.

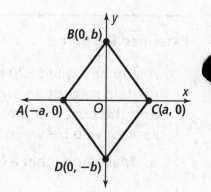

a. How do you know that $ABCD$ is a parallelogram?

b. How do you know that the diagonals of $ABCD$ are perpendicular?

c. How do you know that $ABCD$ can represent any parallelogram with perpendicular diagonals?

d. What must you show to prove that $ABCD$ is a rhombus? What formula can you use?

Standards Practice Week 23

Selected Response

1. Which of the following describes the circle represented by the following equation?

$$(x - 15)^2 + (y + 13)^2 = 64$$

Ⓐ center (15, –13), radius 8

Ⓑ center (–15, 13), radius 64

Ⓒ center (15, –13), radius 64

Ⓓ center (–15, 13), radius 8

Constructed Response

2. What is an equation for the set of points in the coordinate plane that are equidistant from the point (3, –2) and the line $y = -6$? What is the shape of the set of points called?

Extended Response

3. Keenan and Andrew each have a two-way radio with a range of 20 miles.

a. Their locations are represented in a coordinate plane with Keenan at the origin and Andrew at (12, 13). The distance in the coordinate is in miles. Write equations to describe the maximum range of each.

b. Are they within range of each other? Explain.

c. Yumiko also has two-way radio with a range of 20 miles and is at the location (17, –7). Is she in the range for both Keenan and Andrew? Explain.

Standards Practice Week 24

Selected Response

1. $\overline{AB}$ is tangent to ⊙C. What is radius of ⊙C? Round to the nearest tenth.

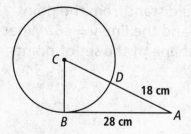

(A) 10.0 cm

(B) 12.8 cm

(C) 15.2 cm

(D) 21.4 cm

Constructed Response

2. The diameter of ⊙P is 24. What is the length of $\overset{\frown}{MN}$? Express the answer in terms of π.

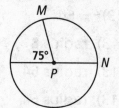

Extended Response

3. Circles A and B each have a radius of 30 in. and $AB = 30$ in.

   a. Draw a diagram that shows both circles.

   b. Find the area of the region that is contained by both circles. Round to the nearest tenth.

Standards Practice Week 25

Selected Response

1. In ⊙E, if diameter $AB = 6$ and $CD = \frac{2}{3}AB$, what is the distance from $\overline{CD}$ to center E?

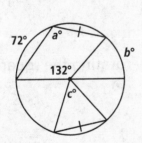

- Ⓐ 1
- Ⓑ $\sqrt{2}$
- Ⓒ $\sqrt{5}$
- Ⓓ $\sqrt{7}$

Constructed Response

2. What is the value of x?

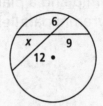

3. What is the value of y?

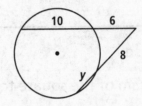

Extended Response

3. Use the diagrams to determine each measure.

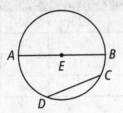 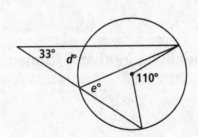 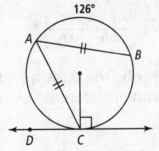

- **a.** $a°$
- **b.** $b°$
- **c.** $c°$
- **d.** $d°$
- **e.** $e°$
- **f.** $m\angle ACD$
- **g.** $m\widehat{BC}$

Standards Practice Week 26

Selected Response

1. What shape is the cross section of a pentagonal pyramid and a plane intersecting the pyramid parallel to the base?

   Ⓐ pentagon

   Ⓑ rectangle

   Ⓒ square

   Ⓓ triangle

Constructed Response

2. Complete the table for each polyhedron.

Polyhedron	Faces	Vertices	Edges
A		20	30
B	10		24
C	13	13	
D	14		36

Extended Response

3. Use the diagram of the square to answer the questions.

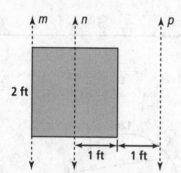

2 ft

1 ft   1 ft

m   n   p

a. Describe the three-dimensional figure that is formed by rotating the square about line *m*.

b. Describe the three-dimensional figure that is formed by rotating the square about line *n*.

c. Describe the three-dimensional figure that is formed by rotating the square about line *p*.

Standards Practice Week 27

Selected Response

1. What is the volume of a cylinder with a diameter of 8 in. and a height of 5 in.? Round your answer to the nearest cubic inch.

   (A) 80 in.^{3}

   (B) 251 in.^{3}

   (C) 640 in.^{3}

   (D) 1,005 in.^{3}

Constructed Response

2. A spherical balloon has a surface area of 50 cm^2. What is the volume of the balloon? Round to the nearest tenth of a cubic centimeter.

Extended Response

3. List these solids in order from the one with the least volume to the one with the greatest volume.

   A a cube with edge 6 cm

   B a cylinder with radius 5 cm and height 6 cm

   C a square pyramid with base edges 9 cm and height 7 cm

   D a cone with radius 6 cm and height 8 cm

   E a rectangular prism with base 6 cm-by-8 cm and height 7 cm

Standards Practice Week 28

Selected Response

1. Events A and B are independent. $P(A) = 0.25$ and $P(B) = 0.40$. What is $P(A \text{ and } B)$?

   Ⓐ 0.10 Ⓒ 0.33

   Ⓑ 0.15 Ⓓ 0.65

2. You roll two standard number cubes. What is the probability of rolling a 4 on one cube but not both cubes?

   Ⓐ $\frac{5}{36}$ Ⓒ $\frac{11}{36}$

   Ⓑ $\frac{5}{18}$ Ⓓ $\frac{1}{3}$

Constructed Response

3. Twelve cards numbered 1 through 12 are placed on a table face down. You select one card and do not return it to the table. Then you select a second card.

   a. Are the events dependent or independent?

   b. What is the probability that both cards show odd numbers?

Extended Response

4. A company asked 500 of its employees if they would rather receive a gift card for a restaurant or a movie theater. Use the information in the table to answer the questions.

Gift Card Preference

	Restaurant	Movie Theater
Female	150	112
Male	124	114

   a. What is the probability that an employee would rather receive a gift card for a movie theater, given that the employee was female?

   b. What is the probability that an employee is male, given that the employee would rather receive a gift card for a restaurant?

Standards Practice Week 29

Selected Response

1. A student chooses at random 5 books from a reading list of 12 books. What is the number of possibilities?

   (A) 60

   (B) 792

   (C) 95,040

   (D) 3,991,680

2. The president, vice-president, and treasurer of a club are chosen from 8 candidates. What is the number of possibilities?

   (A) 24

   (B) 56

   (C) 336

   (D) 6,720

Constructed Response

3. The probability of winning a game is 40%. You play the game 10 times.

   a. What is the probability that you win the game exactly 3 times? Round to the nearest tenth of a percent.

   b. What is the probability that you win the game at least 8 times? Round to the nearest tenth of a percent.

Extended Response

4. The results from a survey of 120 students from City High School are shown.

Number of Children in Household	1	2	3	4	5 or more
Frequency	31	34	24	21	10

   a. Graph the probability distribution based on the survey.

   b. What is the probability that a student lives in a household with 3 or more children?

Standards Practice Week 30

Selected Response

1. One round in a game has four possible outcomes. The table shows the probability and point value for each outcome. What is the expected value for the round?

Outcome	Probability	Points
A	40%	5
B	10%	10
C	20%	−10
D	30%	−5

Ⓐ −0.5

Ⓑ 0

Ⓒ 0.5

Ⓓ 1

Constructed Response

2. Victor and Sadie play a game by each randomly choosing a number from 1 to 4. If the sum of the numbers is prime, Sadie earns the number of points equal to the sum. If the sum of the numbers is not prime, Victor earns the number of points equal to the sum. Is the game fair? If it is unfair, which player has the advantage? Explain.

Extended Response

3. A shuttle service can take 10 riders at a time. The service believes that it is acceptable if it cannot take all riders less than 20% of the time.

    a. If the service has a 22% rate of riders not showing up and takes reservations for 12 riders at a time, would that be acceptable for the service? Explain.

    b. If the rate of riders not showing up increases to 25% and the service still takes reservations for 12 riders at a time, would that be acceptable for the service? Explain.

enVision Geometry

PearsonRealize.com

Practice Test Form A

Part I: Calculator NOT Permitted

1. What value of x makes △ABC similar to △DEF?

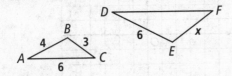

Ⓐ 4.5

Ⓑ 6

Ⓒ 7.5

Ⓓ 8

2. Which equation is an equation of a circle with center (2, −1) passing through the point (−1, 1)?

Ⓐ $(x + 2)^2 + (x − 1)^2 = 13$

Ⓑ $(x − 2)^2 + (x + 1)^2 = 25$

Ⓒ $(x − 2)^2 + (x + 1)^2 = 13$

Ⓓ $(x + 2)^2 + (x − 1)^2 = 25$

3. Complete the table by writing an expression for each trigonometric ratio.

cos 38°	
sin 38°	
cos 52°	
sin 52°	

4. Which theorem can you use to prove that the two triangles are congruent? Select all that apply.

Ⓐ ASA

Ⓑ AAS

Ⓒ HL

Ⓓ SAS

Ⓔ SSS

5. Which shape is formed by a plane perpendicular to the base and intersecting the right pyramid through the top vertex?

Ⓐ pentagon

Ⓑ rectangle

Ⓒ trapezoid

Ⓓ triangle

6. Which angle pair is supplementary? Select all that apply.

Ⓐ ∠1 and ∠5

Ⓑ ∠1 and ∠6

Ⓒ ∠2 and ∠5

Ⓓ ∠3 and ∠6

Ⓔ ∠4 and ∠7

7. What are the coordinates of the point $\frac{2}{3}$ of the way from A(−3, 6) and B(6, −30)?

Ⓐ (3, −18)   Ⓒ (0, −6)

Ⓑ (0, −18)   Ⓓ (2, −16)

8. A dilation maps $\triangle TUV$ to $\triangle T'U'V'$. Which statement must be true?

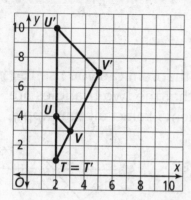

	Yes	No
The center of dilation is O.	❏	❏
The scale factor is 2.	❏	❏
$\overline{UV} \parallel \overline{U'V'}$	❏	❏
$\dfrac{TU}{T'U'} = \dfrac{TV}{T'V'}$	❏	❏

9. Quadrilateral *GHJK* is a parallelogram. What are the values of *x* and *y*?

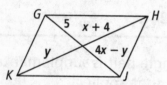

Ⓐ $x = 2.5$, $y = 5$

Ⓑ $x = 3$, $y = 7$

Ⓒ $x = 0.5$, $y = 3.5$

Ⓓ $x = 5$, $y = 7$

10. The center of the inscribed circle of a triangle is located at the

_____ of the triangle, which is the point of concurrency of the

_____ of the triangle.

11. Quadrilateral *LMNP* has vertices $L(4, 4)$, $M(4, -3)$, $N(2, -1)$, and $P(2, 2)$. Graph the image $r_{(90°, O)}(LMNP)$.

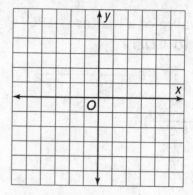

12. Which equation represents a line that contains the point $(8, -3)$ and is perpendicular to $y = 4x - 8$?

Ⓐ $y = -\dfrac{1}{4}x + 2$

Ⓑ $y = -4x + 29$

Ⓒ $y = \dfrac{1}{4}x - 5$

Ⓓ $y = -\dfrac{1}{4}x - 1$

13. Triangle *QRS* is reflected across line *m*. Which statement must be true?

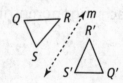

	Yes	No
$m\angle Q' \cong m\angle Q$	❏	❏
$m \perp \overline{RR'}$	❏	❏
$\overline{RR'} \cong \overline{SS'}$	❏	❏
$\overline{RS} \cong \overline{R'S'}$	❏	❏

Short Response

14. Draw the lines of symmetry and give the angles of rotation for the rhombus.

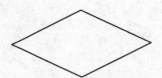

15. A jar contains 10 marbles. Four are blue and 6 are red. What is the probability of selecting two marbles of the same color?

16. Describe a rigid motion or composition of rigid motions that maps △ABC to △DEF.

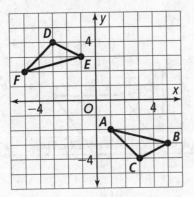

17. The diagonals of a parallelogram are congruent. Classify the parallelogram as specifically as possible.

18. What is the definition of a line segment?

19. Draw and label a 180° rotation of triangle XYZ about point Z. Then describe in terms of rigid motions how XZY and its image are congruent.

20. Describe a similarity transformation that maps ⊙J to ⊙K. Include the scale factor.

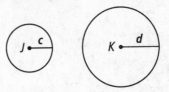

21. Construct the perpendicular bisector of $\overline{FG}$.

F •————————• G

22. Write a congruence statement relating the triangles in the figure, and describe a rigid motion that maps one triangle to the other.

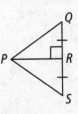

Extended Response

23. Write a proof of the Vertical Angles Theorem.

    Given: ∠1 and ∠2 are vertical angles.
    Prove: ∠1 ≅ ∠2

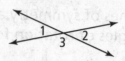

24. Write a proof of the Triangle Exterior Angle Theorem.

    Given: ∠1 is an exterior angle.
    Prove: $m\angle 1 = m\angle 2 + m\angle 3$

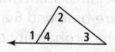

25. Use the diagram to write a coordinate proof to show diagonals of a rhombus are perpendicular.

    Given: rhombus *ABCD*
    Prove: $\overline{AC} \perp \overline{BD}$

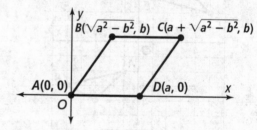

Practice Test Form A

Part II: Calculator Permitted

26. What is the value of x?

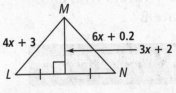

- (A) 0.6
- (B) 1
- (C) 1.4
- (D) 1.6

27. A park provides free train rides on two concentric circular tracks. The distance from track 1 to the center is 30 m. The distance between track 1 and track 2 is 5 m. A pathway with endpoints on track 2 is tangent to track 1. How long is the pathway?

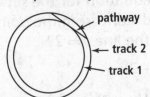

- (A) 18.0 m
- (B) 36.1 m
- (C) 59.2 m
- (D) 60.0 m

28. Which statement must be true? Select all that apply.

- (A) $\cos P = \cos Q$
- (B) $\cos P = \sin Q$
- (C) $\sin P = \sin Q$
- (D) $\sin P = \cos Q$

29. What is the value of x?

- (A) 1.25
- (B) 1.5
- (C) 2.4
- (D) 3.25

30. Complete the table by finding the unknown measures. Round to the nearest tenth.

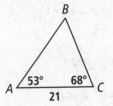

$m\angle B$	
AB	
BC	

31. The eyes of a student standing at the edge of a platform are 8 ft above the ground. She sees a wallet on the ground at an angle of depression of 32°. About how far away from the base of the platform is the wallet?

- (A) 4.2 ft
- (B) 5.0 ft
- (C) 12.8 ft
- (D) 15.1 ft

32. What is the area of the triangle? Round to the nearest tenth.

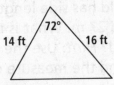

- (A) 34.6 ft²
- (B) 53.3 ft²
- (C) 106.5 ft²
- (D) 344.7 ft²

33. What is the volume of a cone with diameter 12 in. and height 16 in.?

- (A) 603.2 in.³
- (B) 1,809.6 in.³
- (C) 2,412.7 in.³
- (D) 7,238.2 in.³

34. Which statement is sufficient to show that a similarity transformation exists that maps △LMN to △L′M′N′? Select all that apply.

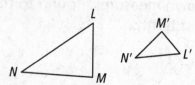

Ⓐ $\angle L \cong \angle L'$, $\angle N \cong \angle N'$

Ⓑ $\frac{LN}{L'N'} = \frac{MN}{M'N''}$, $\angle M \cong \angle M'$

Ⓒ $\frac{LM}{L'M'} = \frac{LN}{L'N'} = \frac{MN}{M'N'}$

Ⓓ $\overline{LL'} \parallel \overline{MM} \parallel \overline{NN'}$

Ⓔ $m\angle M = m\angle M'$, $m\angle N = m\angle N'$

---

35. What is the value of x?

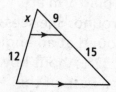

Ⓐ 11.25

Ⓑ 7.2

Ⓒ 6

Ⓓ 4.5

---

36. A triangular field has side lengths 24 m, 15 m, and 27 m. What is the area of the field? *Hint*: Use the Law of Cosines to find the measure of an included angle.

Ⓐ 18 m^2

Ⓑ 179 m^2

Ⓒ 358 m^2

Ⓓ 895 m^2

---

37. The two-way frequency table is incomplete. It shows the results of a town election for mayor. Candidate A won the election by 23 votes. What is the number of Ward 1 voters who chose Candidate B?

	Candidate A	Candidate B
Ward 1 Votes	101	
Ward 2 Votes	97	85

Ⓐ 78

Ⓑ 90

Ⓒ 108

Ⓓ 124

---

38. What is an equation for the set of points equidistant from the point $(-2, 4)$ and the line $y = 2$?

Ⓐ $y = \frac{1}{4}(x + 2)^2$

Ⓑ $y - 3 = \frac{1}{8}(x + 2)^2$

Ⓒ $y - 3 = \frac{1}{4}(x + 2)^2$

Ⓓ $y + 3 = \frac{1}{8}(x - 2)^2$

---

39. A bar of silver is shaped like a trapezoidal prism. The dimensions of the base are shown in the diagram. If the height of the bar is 15 cm, what is its volume to the nearest tenth?

Ⓐ 3,008.4 cm^3

Ⓑ 3,312 cm^3

Ⓒ 4,550.4 cm^3

Ⓓ 4,664.4 cm^3

19.6 cm

9.2 cm

24 cm

Short Response

40. What are the length of $\widehat{MN}$ and the area of sector *MNP*? Round to the nearest tenth.

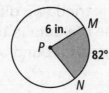

41. A cheer group is making signs for an upcoming rally. They want the signs to be equilateral triangles with heights of 42 in. How long in inches will each side of the signs be? Round to the nearest tenth of an inch.

42. What is the perimeter and area of $\triangle RST$ to the nearest tenth?

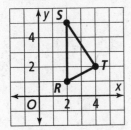

43. What is the density in grams per milliliter of a can of tomato paste with diameter 5.4 cm, height 8.9 cm, and a mass of 150 grams? Use the conversion factor $1 \text{ cm}^3 = 1 \text{ mL}$. Round to the nearest hundredth.

44. What is the perimeter of a right triangle whose hypotenuse has length 10 and whose acute angles measure 29° and 61°? Round to the nearest tenth.

45. Which cylindrical container has a greater volume? How much greater? Round to the nearest cubic inch.

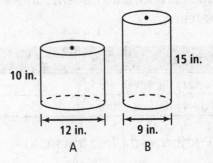

46. Is the dilation $D_{(n,\,A)}(\triangle ABC) = \triangle A'B'C'$ an enlargement or a reduction? What is the scale factor *n*?

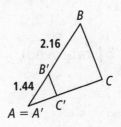

47. Suppose $m\widehat{BCD} = 196°$ and $m\widehat{ADC} = 224°$. What are $m\angle A$, $m\angle B$, $m\angle C$, and $m\angle D$?

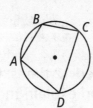

Extended Response

48. In a study to improve memory, researchers tried two different treatment plans to see whether scores improved. Use the data in the table to find the probability of each event. Show your work and round to the nearest tenth of a percent.

	Treatment A	Treatment B
Memory improved	57	46
Memory did not improve	43	34

a. $P(\text{Improved} \mid \text{Treatment A})$

b. $P(\text{Treatment A} \mid \text{Did not improve})$

c. $P(\text{Did not improve} \mid \text{Treatment B})$

d. $P(\text{Treatment B} \mid \text{Improved})$

49. The figure shows a pyramid inscribed in a cube. The volume of the pyramid is 576 cm^3. Find the volume of the cube, and explain the relationship between the volume of the cube and the volume of the pyramid. Then find the length of an edge of the cube.

50. If a fair coin is flipped 12 times, find the probability that either 5, 6, or 7 of the results are heads and explain the method used to find the answer. Round to the nearest ten-thousandth.

Practice Test Form A

Performance Assessment: Designing a Container

Complete this performance task in the space provided. Fully answer all parts of the performance task with detailed responses. You should provide sound mathematical reasoning to support your work.

Three teams of students are designing containers that will hold 2,000 mL of liquid. The containers must be 20 cm high and be open at the top. The shapes that the teams plan to use for their containers are listed below.

- Team 1: rectangular prism with a square base
- Team 2: cylinder
- Team 3: cone (the cone is open at the base)

Task Description

Which team needs the least amount of material to make its container? Which team needs the most material? (Recall that 1 mL = 1 cm^3. Round to the nearest hundredth.)

a. What are the dimensions of Team 1's container? Considering the outside of the container only, what is the surface area?

b. What are the dimensions and surface area of Team 2's container? The lateral surface area of a cylinder is given by the formula L.A. $= 2\pi rh$, where r is the radius of the cylinder and h is the height of the cylinder.

c. What are the dimensions and surface area of Team 3's container? The lateral surface area of the cone is given by the formula L.A. $= \pi r \sqrt{r^2 + h^2}$, where r is the radius of the cone and h is the height of the cone.

d. Which team needs the least amount of material to make its container? Which team needs the most?

e. Suppose Team 2's cylindrical container does not have to be 20 cm high. Can you change the container's dimensions to use less material but still hold 2,000 mL of liquid? Show your work.

Name _____

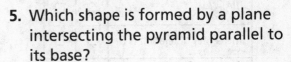
Practice Test Form B

Part I: Calculator NOT Permitted

1. What value of x makes △ABC similar to △DEF?

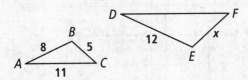

Ⓐ 5

Ⓑ 7.5

Ⓒ 10

Ⓓ 16,5

2. Which equation is an equation of a circle with center (3, −2) passing through the point (−2, 2)?

Ⓐ $(x + 3)^2 + (x − 2)^2 = 41$

Ⓑ $(x − 3)^2 + (x + 2)^2 = 41$

Ⓒ $(x − 3)^2 + (x + 2)^2 = 25$

Ⓓ $(x + 3)^2 + (x − 2)^2 = 25$

3. Complete the table by writing an expression for each trigonometric ratio.

sin 40°	
cos 40°	
sin 50°	
cos 50°	

4. Which theorem can you use to prove that the two triangles are congruent? Select all that apply.

Ⓐ SSS

Ⓑ SAS

Ⓒ HL

Ⓓ AAS

Ⓔ ASA

5. Which shape is formed by a plane intersecting the pyramid parallel to its base?

Ⓐ pentagon

Ⓑ rectangle

Ⓒ trapezoid

Ⓓ triangle

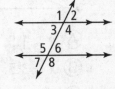

6. Which angles are congruent? Select all that apply.

Ⓐ ∠1 and ∠5

Ⓑ ∠1 and ∠6

Ⓒ ∠2 and ∠5

Ⓓ ∠3 and ∠6

Ⓔ ∠4 and ∠7

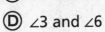

7. What are the coordinates of the point $\frac{1}{3}$ of the way from A(−3, 6) and B(6, −30)?

Ⓐ (3, −18)   Ⓒ (0, −6)

Ⓑ (0, −18)   Ⓓ (2, −16)

8. A dilation maps △TUV to △T'U'V'. Which statement must be true?

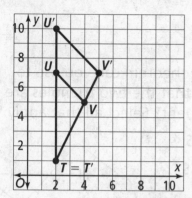

	Yes	No
The scale factor is 1.5.	☐	☐
$\overline{UV} \parallel \overline{U'V'}$	☐	☐
The center of dilation is O.	☐	☐
$\dfrac{TU}{T'U'} = \dfrac{TV}{T'V'}$	☐	☐

9. Quadrilateral *GHJK* is a parallelogram. What are the values of *x* and *y*?

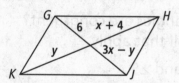

Ⓐ $x = 1.5$, $y = 5.5$

Ⓑ $x = 3.5$, $y = 6$

Ⓒ $x = 5$, $y = 9$

Ⓓ $x = 6$, $y = 10$

10. The center of the circumscribed circle of a triangle is located at the _____ of the triangle, which is the point of concurrency of the _____ _____ of the sides of the triangle.

11. Quadrilateral *LMNP* has vertices $L(4, 4)$, $M(4, -3)$, $N(2, -1)$, and $P(2, 2)$. Graph the image $r_{(180°, O)}(LMNP)$.

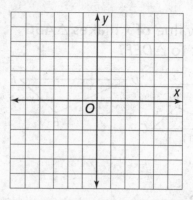

12. Which equation represents a line that contains the point $(8, 7)$ and is perpendicular to $y = 4x - 8$?

Ⓐ $y = -\dfrac{1}{4}x + 9$

Ⓑ $y = -4x + 39$

Ⓒ $y = \dfrac{1}{4} + 7$

Ⓓ $y = -\dfrac{1}{4}x$

13. Triangle *QRS* is reflected across line *m*. Which statement must be true?

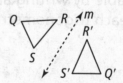

	Yes	No
$\overline{SS'} \cong \overline{RR'}$	☐	☐
$m \perp \overline{QQ'}$	☐	☐
$m\angle R' \cong m\angle R$	☐	☐
$\overline{QR} \cong \overline{Q'S'}$	☐	☐

Short Response

14. Draw the lines of symmetry and give the angles of rotation for the rhombus.

15. A jar contains 10 marbles. Three are blue and 7 are red. What is the probability of selecting two marbles of the same color?

16. Describe a rigid motion or composition of rigid motions that maps △*ABC* to △*DEF*.

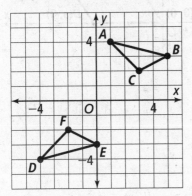

17. The diagonals of a parallelogram are perpendicular and congruent. Classify the parallelogram as specifically as possible.

18. What is the definition of a ray?

19. Draw and label a 180° rotation of triangle *XYZ* about point *X*. Then describe in terms of rigid motions how *XZY* and its image are congruent.

20. Describe a similarity transformation that maps ⊙*G* to ⊙*H*. Include the scale factor.

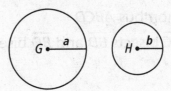

21. Construct the angle bisector of ∠*ABC*.

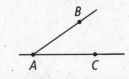

22. Write a congruence statement relating the triangles in the figure and describe a rigid motion that maps one triangle to the other.

Extended Response

23. Write a proof of the Congruent Supplements Theorem.

    Given: $m\angle 1 + m\angle 2 = 180°$, $m\angle 2 + m\angle 3 = 180°$

    Prove: $\angle 1 \cong \angle 3$

    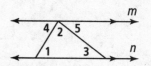

24. Write a proof of the Triangle Angle-Sum Theorem.

    Given: $m \parallel n$

    Prove: $m\angle 1 + m\angle 2 + m\angle 3 = 180°$

    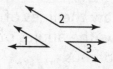

25. Use the diagram to write a coordinate proof to show diagonals of a rhombus bisect each other.

    Given: rhombus *ABCD*

    Prove: $\overline{AC}$ bisects $\overline{BD}$ and $\overline{BD}$ bisects $\overline{AC}$

    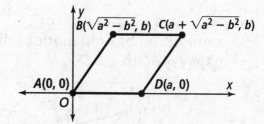

Practice Test Form B

Part II: Calculator Permitted

26. What is *LM*?

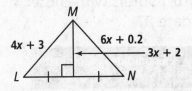

(A) 5.4   (C) 8.6

(B) 7   (D) 9.4

27. A park provides free train rides on two concentric circular tracks. The distance from track 1 to the center is 60 m. The distance between track 1 and track 2 is 10 m. A pathway with endpoints on track 2 is tangent to track 1. How long is the pathway?

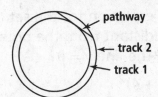

(A) 36.0 m   (C) 128.4 m

(B) 72.2 m   (D) 120.0 m

28. Which statement must be true? Select all that apply.

(A) $\sin A = \cos B$

(B) $\sin A = \sin B$

(C) $\cos A = \sin B$

(D) $\cos A = \cos B$

29. What is the value of *x*?

(A) 2.5

(B) 3

(C) 4.8

(D) 6.5

30. Complete the table by finding the unknown measures. Round to the nearest tenth.

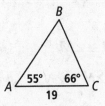

$m\angle B$	
AB	
BC	

31. The eyes of a student standing at the edge of a platform are 8 ft above the ground. She sees a wallet on the ground at an angle of depression of 32°. About how far away from the base of the platform is the wallet?

(A) 5.3 ft   (C) 16.0 ft

(B) 6.3 ft   (D) 18.9 ft

32. What is the area of the triangle? Round to the nearest tenth.

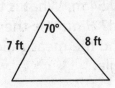

(A) 7.0 ft²   (C) 26.3 ft²

(B) 14.1 ft²   (D) 52.6 ft²

33. What is the volume of a cone with diameter 6 in. and height 8 in.?

(A) 75.4 in.³   (C) 301.6 in.³

(B) 226.2 in.³   (D) 904.8 in.³

34. Which statement is sufficient to show that a similarity transformation exists that maps $\triangle LMN$ to $\triangle L'M'N'$? Select all that apply.

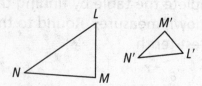

Ⓐ $\angle L \cong \angle L'$, $\angle M \cong \angle M'$

Ⓑ $\dfrac{LN}{L'N'} = \dfrac{MN}{M'N'}$, $\angle N \cong \angle N'$

Ⓒ $\dfrac{LM}{L'M'} = \dfrac{LN}{L'N'} = \dfrac{MN}{M'N'}$

Ⓓ $\overline{LL'} \parallel \overline{MM} \parallel \overline{NN'}$

Ⓔ $m\angle L = m\angle L'$, $m\angle N = m\angle N'$

---

35. What is the value of x?

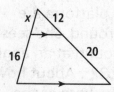

Ⓐ 4.8

Ⓑ 8

Ⓒ 9.6

Ⓓ 15

---

36. A triangular field has side lengths 48 m, 30 m, and 54 m. What is the area of the field? *Hint:* Use the Law of Cosines to find the measure of an included angle.

Ⓐ 72 m²

Ⓑ 716 m²

Ⓒ 1,432 m²

Ⓓ 3,580 m²

---

37. The two-way frequency table is incomplete. It shows the results of a town election for mayor. Candidate A won the election by 46 votes. What is the number of Ward 1 voters who chose Candidate B?

	Candidate A	Candidate B
Ward 1 Votes	202	
Ward 2 Votes	194	170

Ⓐ 156

Ⓑ 180

Ⓒ 216

Ⓓ 248

---

38. What is an equation for the set of points equidistant from the point $(-4, 2)$ and the line $y = 0$?

Ⓐ $y = \dfrac{1}{4}(x + 4)^2$

Ⓑ $y - 1 = \dfrac{1}{8}(x + 4)^2$

Ⓒ $y - 1 = \dfrac{1}{4}(x + 4)^2$

Ⓓ $y + 1 = \dfrac{1}{8}(x - 4)^2$

---

39. A bar of silver is shaped like a trapezoidal prism. The dimensions of the base are shown in the diagram. If the height of the bar is 20 cm, what is its volume to the nearest cubic centimeter?

Ⓐ 1,800 cm³

Ⓑ 3,240 cm³

Ⓒ 3,600 cm³

Ⓓ 6,480 cm³

16 cm
9 cm
20 cm

Short Response

40. What are the length of $\widehat{MN}$ and the area of sector MNP? Round to the nearest tenth.

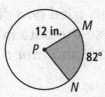

12 in.

M

P

82°

N

41. A cheer group is making signs for an upcoming rally. They want the signs to be equilateral triangles with heights of 36 in. How long in inches will each side of the signs be? Round to the nearest tenth of an inch.

42. What is the perimeter and area of △RST to the nearest tenth?

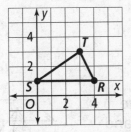

43. What is the density in grams per milliliter of a can of tomato paste with diameter 5.5 cm, height 10.1 cm, and a mass of 170 grams? Use the conversion factor 1 cm^3 = 1 mL. Round to the nearest hundredth.

44. What is the perimeter of a right triangle whose hypotenuse has length 12 and whose acute angles measure 29° and 61°? Round to the nearest tenth.

45. Which cylindrical container has a greater volume? How much greater? Round to the nearest cubic inch.

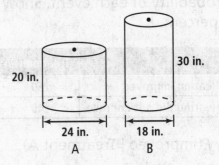

20 in.

30 in.

24 in.
A

18 in.
B

46. Is the dilation $D_{(n, A)}(\triangle ABC) = \triangle A'B'C'$ an enlargement or a reduction? What is the scale factor n?

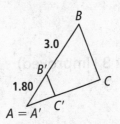

B

3.0

B'

1.80

C

C'

A = A'

47. Suppose $m\widehat{BCD} = 192°$ and $m\widehat{ADC} = 228°$. What are m∠A, m∠B, m∠C, and m∠D?

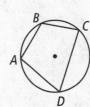

B

C

A

D

Extended Response

48. In a study to improve hearing, researchers tried two different treatment plans to see whether scores improved. Use the data in the table to find the probability of each event. Show your work and round to the nearest tenth of a percent.

	Treatment A	Treatment B
Hearing improved	60	49
Hearing did not improve	40	31

a. P(Improved | Treatment A)

b. P(Treatment A | Did not Improve)

c. P(Did not improve | Treatment B)

d. P(Treatment B | Improved)

49. The figure shows a pyramid inscribed in a cube. The volume of the pyramid is 1,125 cm^3. Find the volume of the cube, and explain the relationship between the volume of the cube and the volume of the pyramid. Then find the length of an edge of the cube.

50. If a fair coin is flipped 20 times, find the probability that either 9, 10, or 11 of the results are heads and explain the method used to find the answer. Round to the nearest ten-thousandth.

Practice Test Form B

Performance Assessment: Urban Planning

Complete this performance task in the space provided. Fully answer all parts of the performance task with detailed responses. You should provide sound mathematical reasoning to support your work.

Students are designing a new town as part of a social studies project on urban planning. They want to place the town's high school at point *A* and the middle school at point *B*. They also plan to build roads that run directly from point *A* to the mall and from point *B* to the mall. The average cost to build a road in this area is $600,000 per mile.

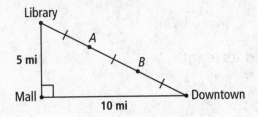

Task Description

What is the difference in the cost of the roads built to the mall for the two schools?

a. Find the measure of each acute angle of the right triangle shown.

b. Find the length of the hypotenuse. Also find the length of each of the three congruent segments forming the hypotenuse.

c. Draw the road from point A to the mall, and find its length.

d. Draw the road from point B to the mall, and find its length.

e. How much farther from the mall is point B than point A? How much more will it cost to build the longer road?

Practice Test Form C

Part I: Calculator NOT Permitted

1. What value of x makes △ABC similar to △DEF?

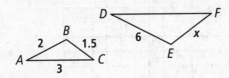

Ⓐ 3

Ⓑ 6

Ⓒ 4.5

Ⓓ 12

2. Which equation is an equation of a circle with center (−3, 2) passing through the point (2, −2)?

Ⓐ $(x + 3)^2 + (x − 2)^2 = 41$

Ⓑ $(x − 3)^2 + (x + 2)^2 = 41$

Ⓒ $(x − 3)^2 + (x + 2)^2 = 25$

Ⓓ $(x + 3)^2 + (x − 2)^2 = 25$

3. Complete the table by writing an expression for each trigonometric ratio.

sin 36°	
cos 36°	
sin 54°	
cos 54°	

4. Which theorem can you use to prove that the two triangles are congruent? Select all that apply.

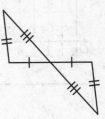

Ⓐ AAS

Ⓑ ASA

Ⓒ HL

Ⓓ SSS

Ⓔ SAS

5. Which shape is formed by a plane intersecting the pyramid parallel to its base?

Ⓐ hexagon

Ⓑ rectangle

Ⓒ trapezoid

Ⓓ triangle

6. Which pairs of angles are not congruent? Select all that apply.

Ⓐ ∠1 and ∠5

Ⓑ ∠1 and ∠6

Ⓒ ∠2 and ∠5

Ⓓ ∠3 and ∠6

Ⓔ ∠4 and ∠7

7. What are the coordinates of the point $\frac{1}{4}$ of the way from A(−4, 6) and B(8, −30)?

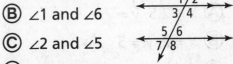

Ⓐ (4, −24) Ⓒ (2, −12)

Ⓑ (−2, −3) Ⓓ (5, −21)

8. A dilation maps △*TUV* to △*T'U'V'*. Which statement must be true?

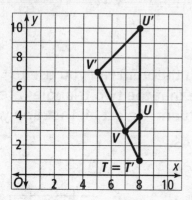

	Yes	No
The scale factor is 3.	❑	❑
$\overline{UU'} \cong \overline{VV'}$	❑	❑
The center of dilation is *O*.	❑	❑
$\frac{UV}{U'V'} = \frac{TV}{T'V'}$	❑	❑

9. Quadrilateral *GHJK* is a parallelogram. What are the values of *x* and *y*?

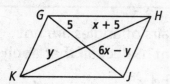

Ⓐ *x* = 2.5, *y* = 7.5

Ⓑ *x* = 2, *y* = 5

Ⓒ *x* = 2, *y* = 7

Ⓓ *x* = 0, *y* = 5

10. A triangle will balance on a point if the point is placed at the _____ of the triangle, which is the point of concurrency of the _____ of the triangle.

11. Quadrilateral *LMNP* has vertices *L*(4, 4), *M*(4, −3), *N*(2, −1), and *P*(2, 2). Graph the image $r_{(270°, O)}$ (*LMNP*).

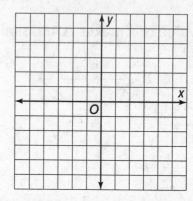

12. Which equation represents a line that contains the point (16, 5) and is perpendicular to *y* = 4*x* − 8?

Ⓐ $y = \frac{1}{4}x + 1$

Ⓑ $y = -\frac{1}{4}x + 9$

Ⓒ $y = -4x + 69$

Ⓓ $y = -\frac{1}{4}x + 5$

13. Triangle *QRS* is reflected across line *m*. Which statement must be true?

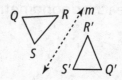

	Yes	No
$\overline{QQ'} \parallel \overline{RR'}$	❑	❑
$m \perp \overline{QQ'}$	❑	❑
$m\angle S' \cong m\angle S$	❑	❑
$\overline{QR} \cong \overline{Q'S'}$	❑	❑

Short Response

14. Draw the lines of symmetry, and give the angles of rotation for the equilateral triangle.

15. A jar contains 10 marbles. Five are blue and 5 are red. What is the probability of selecting two marbles of the same color?

16. Describe a rigid motion or composition of rigid motions that maps △*ABC* to △*DEF*.

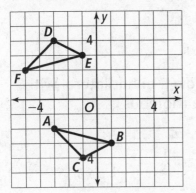

17. The diagonals of a parallelogram are perpendicular. Classify the parallelogram as specifically as possible.

18. What is the definition of an angle?

19. Draw and label a 180° rotation of triangle *XYZ* about point *Y*. Then describe in terms of rigid motions how *XZY* and its image are congruent.

20. Describe a similarity transformation that maps ⊙*K* to ⊙*J*. Include the scale factor.

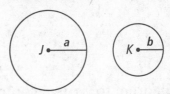

21. Construct $\overline{CD}$ congruent to $\overline{AB}$.

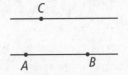

22. Write a congruence statement relating the triangles in the figure, and describe a rigid motion that maps one triangle to the other.

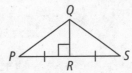

Extended Response

23. Write a proof of the Congruent Complements Theorem.

Given: $m\angle 1 + m\angle 2 = 90°$, $m\angle 2 + m\angle 3 = 90°$
Prove: $\angle 1 \cong \angle 3$

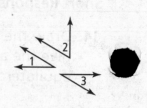

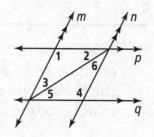

24. Write a proof to show that two angles are congruent.

Given: $m \parallel n$ and $p \parallel q$
Prove: $\angle 1 \cong \angle 4$

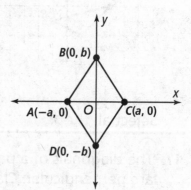

25. Use the diagram to write a coordinate proof to show a quadrilateral with perpendicular diagonals that bisect each other is a rhombus.

Given: $\overline{AC} \perp \overline{BD}$; $\overline{AC}$ and $\overline{BD}$ bisect each other.
Prove: $ABCD$ is a rhombus.

Practice Test Form C

Part II: Calculator Permitted

26. What is the altitude of $\triangle LMN$ to vertex M?

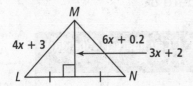

- (A) 3.8
- (C) 6.2
- (B) 5
- (D) 6.8

27. A park provides free train rides on two concentric circular tracks. The distance from track 1 to the center is 15 m. The distance between track 1 and track 2 is 2.5 m. A pathway with endpoints on track 2 is tangent to track 1. How long is the pathway?

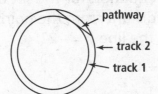

- (A) 9.0 m
- (C) 32.1 m
- (B) 18.1 m
- (D) 30.0 m

28. Which statement must be true? Select all that apply.

- (A) $\cos D = \cos E$
- (B) $\sin D = \sin E$
- (C) $\cos D = \sin E$
- (D) $\sin D = \cos E$

29. What is the value of x?

- (A) 5
- (B) 6
- (C) 9.6
- (D) 11

30. Complete the table by finding the unknown measures. Round to the nearest tenth.

$m\angle B$	
AB	
BC	

31. The eyes of a student standing at the edge of a platform are 12 ft above the ground. She sees a wallet on the ground at an angle of depression of 32°. About how far away from the base of the platform is the wallet?

- (A) 6.4 ft
- (C) 19.2 ft
- (B) 7.6 ft
- (D) 22.7 ft

32. What is the area of the triangle? Round to the nearest tenth.

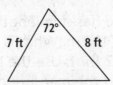

- (A) 8.7 ft²
- (C) 26.6 ft²
- (B) 13.3 ft²
- (D) 86.2 ft²

33. What is the volume of a cone with diameter 24 in. and height 32 in.?

- (A) 4,825 in.³
- (C) 19,302 in.³
- (B) 14,476 in.³
- (D) 57,906 in.³

34. Which statement is sufficient to show that a similarity transformation exists that maps △LMN to △L′M′N′? Select all that apply.

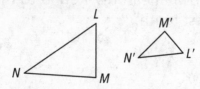

Ⓐ $\dfrac{LM}{L'M'} = \dfrac{LN}{L'N'} = \dfrac{MN}{M'N'}$

Ⓑ $\dfrac{LN}{L'N'} = \dfrac{MN}{M'N'}$, $\angle L \cong \angle L'$

Ⓒ $\angle M \cong \angle M'$, $\angle N \cong N'$

Ⓓ $\overline{LL'} \parallel \overline{MM} \parallel \overline{NN'}$

Ⓔ $m\angle L = m\angle L'$, $m\angle M = m\angle M'$

---

35. What is the value of x?

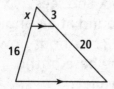

Ⓐ 2.4

Ⓑ 3.75

Ⓒ 4.8

Ⓓ 6

---

36. A triangular field has side lengths 96 m, 60 m, and 108 m. What is the area of the field? *Hint:* Use the Law of Cosines to find the measure of an included angle.

Ⓐ 288 m²

Ⓑ 2,864 m²

Ⓒ 5,728 m²

Ⓓ 14,320 m²

---

37. The two-way frequency table is incomplete. It shows the results of a town election for mayor. Candidate A won the election by 92 votes. What is the number of Ward 1 Voters who chose Candidate B?

	Candidate A	Candidate B
Ward 1 Votes	404	
Ward 2 Votes	388	340

Ⓐ 312

Ⓑ 360

Ⓒ 432

Ⓓ 496

---

38. What is an equation for the set of points equidistant from the point (−8, 0) and the line $y = -2$?

Ⓐ $y = \dfrac{1}{4}(x + 8)^2$

Ⓑ $y - 1 = \dfrac{1}{8}(x + 8)^2$

Ⓒ $y + 1 = \dfrac{1}{4}(x + 8)^2$

Ⓓ $y + 1 = \dfrac{1}{8}(x - 8)^2$

---

39. A bar of silver is shaped like a trapezoidal prism. The dimensions of the base are shown in the diagram. If the height of the bar is 10 cm, what is its volume to the nearest cubic centimeter?

Ⓐ 3,240 cm³

Ⓑ 1,800 cm³

Ⓒ 1,620 cm³

Ⓓ 900 cm³

16 cm

9 cm

20 cm

Short Response

40. What are the length of $\widehat{MN}$ and the area of sector *MNP*? Round to the nearest tenth.

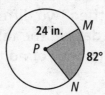

41. A cheer group is making signs for an upcoming rally. They want the signs to be equilateral triangles with heights of 48 in. How long in inches will each side of the signs be? Round to the nearest tenth of an inch.

42. What is the perimeter and area of △*RST* to the nearest tenth?

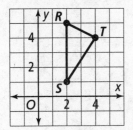

43. What is the density in grams per milliliter of a can of tomato paste with diameter 5.6 cm, height 10.3 cm, and a mass of 170 grams? Use the conversion factor $1 \text{ cm}^3 = 1 \text{ mL}$. Round to the nearest hundredth.

44. What is the perimeter of a right triangle whose hypotenuse has length 8 and whose acute angles measure 29° and 61°? Round to the nearest tenth.

45. Which cylindrical container has a greater volume? How much greater? Round to the nearest cubic inch.

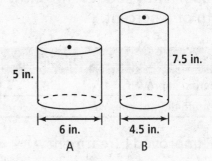

46. Is the dilation $D_{(n,\, A)}(\triangle ABC) = \triangle A'B'C'$ an enlargement or a reduction? What is the scale factor *n*?

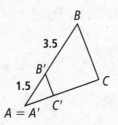

47. Suppose $m\widehat{BCD} = 196°$ and $m\widehat{ADC} = 224°$. What are $m\angle A$, $m\angle B$, $m\angle C$, and $m\angle D$?

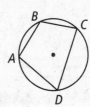

Extended Response

48. In a study to improve vision, researchers tried two different treatment plans to see whether scores improved. Use the data in the table to find the probability of each event. Show your work and round to the nearest tenth of a percent.

	Treatment A	Treatment B
Hearing improved	30	33
Hearing did not improve	70	47

a. P(Improved | Treatment A)

b. P(Treatment A | Did not improve)

c. P(Did not improve | Treatment B)

d. P(Treatment B | Improved)

49. The figure shows a pyramid inscribed in a cube. The volume of the pyramid is 1,944 cm^3. Find the volume of the cube, and explain the relationship between the volume of the cube and the volume of the pyramid. Then find the length of an edge of the cube.

50. If a fair coin is flipped 10 times, find the probability that either 4, 5, or 6 of the results are heads, and explain the method used to find the answer. Round to the nearest ten-thousandth.

Practice Test Form C

Performance Assessment: Analyzing an Excavation Site

Complete this performance task in the space provided. Fully answer all parts of the performance task with detailed responses. You should provide sound mathematical reasoning to support your work.

Archeologists find evidence of three houses at a dig site. They believe the houses were arranged in a circle and want to excavate at the center of the settlement. The map shows the locations of the three houses at points *A*, *B*, and *C*.

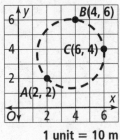

1 unit = 10 m

Task Description

Find the coordinates of the center of the settlement and how far each house was from the center.

a. For any chord of a circle, the perpendicular bisector of the chord passes through the circle's center. Explain how you can use this fact to find the center of the circle.

b. Find the midpoints of $\overline{AB}$ and $\overline{BC}$.

c. Find the slopes of $\overline{AB}$ and $\overline{BC}$.

d. Use the midpoints and slopes of $\overline{AB}$ and $\overline{BC}$ to write equations for the perpendicular bisectors of these segments.

e. What are the coordinates of the settlement's center? Explain.

f. How far was each house from the center of the settlement?

g. Give possible coordinates of another house in the settlement.

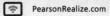

Progress Monitoring for Geometry Practice Tests

Item	Objective	Test A ✓ or ✗	Test B ✓ or ✗	Test C ✓ or ✗	Lesson
1	Use the ratio of corresponding side lengths of similar triangles to solve a problem.				7-2
2	Find an equation of a circle.				9-3
3	Find trigonometric ratios.				8-2
4	Show that triangles are congruent.				4-3
5	Find the cross section of a polyhedron.				11-1
6	Relate angles formed by parallel lines and a transversal.				2-1
7	Find the location of a point by partitioning a segment.				1-3
8	Use properties of a dilation to solve a problem.				7-1
9	Use properties of parallelograms to solve a problem.				6-3
10	Determine the point of concurrency in a triangle.				5-3
11	Graph the image of a rotation.				3-3

Item	Objective	Test A ✓ or X	Test B ✓ or X	Test C ✓ or X	Lesson
12	Find an equation of a perpendicular line.				2-4
13	Understand properties of a reflection.				3-1
14	Determine lines of symmetry and angle measures for rotational symmetry.				3-5
15	Calculate a conditional probability.				12-3
16	Use rigid motions to show that figures are congruent.				4-1
17	Use properties of special quadrilaterals to classify a figure.				6-5
18	Understand precise definitions of geometric figures.				1-1
19	Understand congruence in terms of rigid motions.				4-1
20	Use similarity transformations to show that all circles are similar.				7-2
21	Construct a basic figure.				1-2
22	Use rigid motions to show figures are congruent.				4-1
23	Prove theorems about lines and angles.				1-7
24	Prove theorems about triangles.				2-3

Item	Objective	Test A ✓ or X	Test B ✓ or X	Test C ✓ or X	Lesson
25	Use coordinate geometry to prove theorems.				9-2
26	Understand the properties of a perpendicular bisector.				5-1
27	Use properties of chords and tangents to solve a problem.				10-3
28	Understand the relationship of trigonometric ratios in right triangles.				8-2
29	Use proportions in triangles to solve a problem.				7-5
30	Use the Law of Sines to solve a problem.				8-3
31	Use trigonometry to solve a problem.				8-5
32	Apply trigonometry to find the area of a triangle.				8-5
33	Determine the volume of a cone.				11-3
34	Prove similarity of triangles.				7-3
35	Use proportions in triangles to solve a problem.				7-5
36	Use the Law of Cosines to solve a problem.				8-4
37	Use a two-way frequency table.				12-1

Item	Objective	Test A ✓ or ✗	Test B ✓ or ✗	Test C ✓ or ✗	Lesson
38	Find an equation of a parabola.				9-4
39	Use the volume of a prism to solve a problem.				11-2
40	Find the length of an arc and the area of a sector.				10-1
41	Use special right triangles to solve a problem.				8-1
42	Find perimeters and areas of polygons on the coordinate plane.				9-1
43	Use volumes to solve a problem.				11-2
44	Use trigonometric ratios to solve a problem.				8-2
45	Compare the volumes of solids.				11-2
46	Understand the properties of a dilation.				7-1
47	Use inscribed angles to solve a problem.				10-4
48	Use a two-way frequency table to find probabilities.				12-1
49	Use volumes of prisms and pyramids to solve a problem.				11-3
50	Use probability distributions to solve a problem.				12-5

Table 1 Measures

	United States Customary	Metric
Length	12 inches (in.) = 1 foot (ft) 36 in. = 1 yard (yd) 3 ft = 1 yd 5,280 ft = 1 mile (mi) 1,760 yd = 1 mi	10 mm = 1 centimeter (cm) 100 cm = 1 meter (m) 1,000 mm = 1 m 1,000 m = 1 kilometer (km)
Capacity	8 (fl oz) = 1 cup (c) 2 c = 1 pint (pt) 2 pt = 1 quart (qt) 4 qt = 1 gallon (gal)	1,000 (mL) = 1 liter (L) 1,000 L = 1 kiloliter (kL)
Weight or Mass	16 ounces (oz) = 1 pound (lb) 2,000 lb = 1 ton (t)	1,000 (mg) = 1 gram (g) 1,000 g = 1 kilogram (kg) 1,000 kg = 1 metric ton

	Customary Units and Metric Units
Length	1 in. = 2.54 cm 1 mi ≈ 1.61 km 1 ft ≈ 0.305 m
Capacity	1 qt ≈ 0.946 L
Weight or Mass	1 oz ≈ 28.4 g 1 lb ≈ 0.454 kg

Time	
60 seconds (s) = 1 (min) 60 min = 1 hour (h) 24 h = 1 day (d) 7 d = 1 (wk)	4 weeks = 1 month (mo) 365 d = 1 year (yr) 52 wk = 1 year 12 mo = 1 yr

Formulas of Geometry

Here are some perimeter, area, and volume formulas.	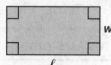 $P = 2l + 2w$ $A = lw$ **Rectangle**	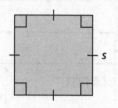 $P = 4s$ $A = s^2$ **Square**
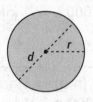 $C = 2\pi r$ or $C = \pi d$ $A = \pi r^2$ **Circle**	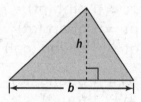 $A = \frac{1}{2}bh$ **Triangle**	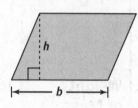 $A = bh$ **Parallelogram**
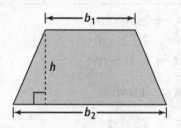 $A = \frac{1}{2}(b_1 + b_2)h$ **Trapezoid**	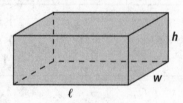 $V = Bh$ $V = lwh$ **Right Prism**	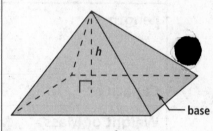 $V = \frac{1}{3}Bh$ **Right Pyramid**
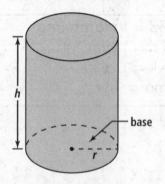 $V = Bh$ $V = \pi r^2 h$ **Right Cylinder**	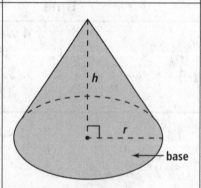 $V = \frac{1}{3}Bh$ $V = \frac{1}{3}\pi r^2 h$ **Right Cone**	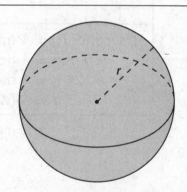 $V = \frac{4}{3}\pi r^3$ **Sphere**